FOR SUCH A TIME
AS THIS

FOR SUCH A TIME AS THIS

PRAYING IN THE LAST DAYS

PATSY CAMENETI

16 15 14 13 12 11   07 06 05 04 03 02

For Such a Time as This
ISBN 13: 978-0-89276-988-9
ISBN 10: 0-89276-988-2

Copyright © 2010 RHEMA Bible Church
AKA Kenneth Hagin Ministries, Inc.
All rights reserved.
Printed in USA

In the U.S. write:
Kenneth Hagin Ministries
P.O. Box 50126
Tulsa, OK 74150-0126
1-888-28-FAITH
www.rhema.org

In Australia write:
Kenneth Hagin Ministries Australia
P.O. Box 6316
Logan Central, QLD 4114
+61 7 3208 6640
www.khm.org.au

Table of Contents

Introduction

For four years my husband, Tony, our daughters, Liliana and Annalisa, and I lived on the island of Singapore. Occasionally we took a cable car to a smaller island called Sentosa. The cable car travels along a strong cable which is securely fastened high above the ground between two grand towers—one on Singapore and the other on Sentosa.

This scene illustrates something of eternal significance for me. There are two major events on God's calendar which give Christians purpose and direction for their lives. One is the First Coming of Jesus; the other is His Second Coming.

When we accept Jesus Christ as our personal Savior, our lives, pictured by the cable, are lifted up from the ground and fastened onto the first tower—the First Coming of Jesus and the redemptive work for which He came. But without the second tower—representing the Second Coming—to attach to, the cable of our lives begins to go downward and we will only live for the here and now. God's purpose for each of us will be lost and we will not reach our destiny.

If we are to ever fully accomplish our God-given destiny, then our lives must be suspended between these two towering events: Jesus' First *and* Second Coming. The purpose of our lives must be fastened and suspended between a consciousness of these two events. May the Lord open our eyes to see and live in the awareness that Jesus not only came, but Jesus is coming again!

My parents, Rev. Bill and Ginger Behrman, are one of my life's greatest blessings. In our church, as well as in our home as I was growing up, they saw to it that the Holy Spirit was always welcome and Jesus was absolutely central. The mission of Jesus' First Coming—His life, ministry, death, and resurrection—was something I was taught and deeply cherished.

Prayer was a significant yet natural part of our life at home. At church, prayer wasn't relegated to a prayer meeting on Tuesday morning with a few faithful folks. Instead it was something all of us did—men, women, teens, and even little children.

I remember many times at the end of a Sunday evening service when prayer was prompted by a desire to be personally ready for Jesus' coming. This same subject also prompted us to pray fervent and heartfelt prayers for our family, friends, school, nation, and world to come to a saving knowledge of Jesus. Many of the young people of that church have since stepped into their roles as church leaders and planters, pastors and missionaries, as part of the answer to those prayers.

The subject of Jesus' return was not only a part of our prayers but was many times the last verse of the songs we sang. We thought about His Second Coming, planned for it, and yearned for the day we would see Him face to face. We lived conscious of the fact that we would stand before Jesus one day regarding what we did in obedience to His will.

This foundation in my life was built upon beautifully under the ministry of Brother Kenneth E. Hagin who I was privileged to serve for 16 years. During those years of study, observation, and participation, my esteem for all the Lord Jesus accomplished when He came the first time was augmented. Oh! What a Savior! Everyone should know Him and all He paid for!

Also throughout those years, there were scores of prayer sessions with Brother Hagin in both large and small settings. During this time, particular things were planted in my heart by the Holy Spirit concerning John the Baptist's ministry of preparing the way for the Lord's coming.

Just as preparation was made for Jesus' First Coming, preparation is being made even now for His Second Coming. There are those who are preparing the way for His return just as John the Baptist did for His First Coming.

The development of this truth within my heart is what has inspired the writing of this book. The scriptures we will look at will give a broader understanding of what is involved in preparing the way for Jesus' return. This understanding will supply light and a solid position from which to pray and will help us cooperate with the Holy Spirit in prayer in these last days.

> *"He who testifies to these things says,*
> *'Surely I am coming quickly.' Amen.*
> *Even so, come, Lord Jesus!"*
>
> —Revelation 22:20

CHAPTER 1

Preparing the Way:
A Voice in the Wilderness

The first advent of Christ was scheduled and planned before the foundation of the earth. He would first come as a lamb—the Lamb, slain.

The first prophecy in the Bible regarding Jesus' coming and a work He would accomplish is found in Genesis 3:15. Various aspects of His coming were prophesied from that time on, over a period of many, many years—line upon line, and prophecy upon prophecy. Finally, He came in the fullness of time (Gal. 4:4).

The first coming of Jesus involved many people who helped prepare the way. We are familiar with the names of those who prophesied about the Messiah, but as the time of Jesus' birth drew near we see various characters, not just the prophets, who were involved in Jesus' coming.

> The first coming of Jesus involved many people who helped prepare the way.

MARY: We see Jesus' mother, Mary. She was a young woman of grace and character. God's hand was obviously upon her in order to prepare her for the amazing role of being Jesus' mother.

JOSEPH: Then there was Joseph, who did not have any biological part in fathering Jesus, but was handpicked by God to help raise Jesus. Someone else of lesser character could have exploited this young prodigy. When Joseph saw how extraordinary Jesus was, he could have used this boy for his own advantage but did not.

OTHER SIGNIFICANT PEOPLE: We see Zechariah and Elizabeth who in their old age also had an important part in the coming of Jesus. Then there were those who came to see the baby Jesus because of signs in the heavens. Following a star, wise men brought significant gifts. Shepherds came to worship after an angelic choir announced Jesus' birth. Each person who was involved in Jesus' First Coming had a role to play and a function to perform in preparing the way of the Lord.

ANNA AND SIMEON: There were also people who prayed. We only see a glimpse of Anna and Simeon at the end of their ministries, yet Anna had prayed for many years. She had given her life since she had been widowed, living in the temple and praying for this event to come to pass. We know Simeon was also devoted to prayer in the temple.

The Second Coming of Jesus will also involve many different people whose functions will be similar to those we have seen in His First Coming. All of these different individuals involved in the First Coming serve as prototypes for the functions of those who are preparing the way for Jesus' Second Coming.

For example, there are many who fit into a similar function as Anna, devoting their lives to prayer. Years ago, I prayed a great deal for "Anna" and at first wondered who it was I was praying about! While I may have been praying for a specific person by that name, I later came to believe that I was praying for those people who fit into the role of giving their lives in a ministry of prayer to help bring back the King!

There is one character, however, which warrants a closer look. This character's role was most unique in the First Coming of Jesus.

The Voice of One Crying in the Wilderness

John the Baptist had a ministry and role in the First Coming of Jesus which was of such great importance that Jesus said there was no prophet ever before John who was greater. With the absence of any recorded miracles (John 10:41), what was it about John's ministry that made him stand above the rest, according to Jesus?

A prophecy given at the time of John's birth through his father, Zechariah, shows us the importance of John's ministry and his direct connection to Jesus' ministry and purpose on earth. *"And you, little one, shall be called a prophet of the Most High; for you shall go on before the face of the Lord to make ready His ways"* (Luke 1:76 Amplified).

The Greek word for *ways* is *hodos*, whose primary meaning is "road."[1] The *Good News Bible* actually translates it that way: *"You will go ahead of the Lord to prepare his road for him"* (Luke 1:76 GNB). In other words, John built a road—a spiritual road that Jesus walked on in ministry.

MARK 1:2–3

2 As it is written in the Prophets: "Behold, I send My messenger before Your face, Who will prepare Your way before You."

3 "The voice of one crying in the wilderness: 'Prepare the way [road] of the Lord; Make His paths straight.' "

Mark was quoting Isaiah, so let's see what Isaiah had to say about road building. *"A voice of one who cries: Prepare in the wilderness the way of the Lord [clear away the obstacles]; make straight and smooth in the desert a highway for our God!"* (Isa. 40:3 Amplified).

Highway in Hebrew is *mecillah*, which means "thoroughfare" or "turnpike."[2] This gives the picture of a main highway, like an interstate.

ISAIAH 40:4-5 (Amplified)

4 Every valley shall be lifted and filled up, and every mountain and hill shall be made low; and the crooked and uneven shall be made straight and level, and the rough places a plain.

5 And the glory (majesty and splendor) of the Lord shall be revealed, and all flesh shall see it together; for the mouth of the Lord has spoken it.

Both sets of my grandparents were pioneers in the state of Colorado in the early 1900s. While Grandpa Behrman was county commissioner, his leadership opened the way for travel from Chaffee County to Gunnison County.

There had been a trail over Cottonwood Pass, which was impassible by automobile. It had been used by wagon freighters with team and wagon decades before. With difficulty, some cars could make it to the top of the pass but could not proceed farther into the beautiful region beyond.

As a young man, my dad remembers the construction work taking place that opened the pass travelers enjoy today. It was through Grandpa's vision, perseverance, and hard work that approval was obtained for construction to begin. Road building was a lot more difficult in those days than it is now with all the great equipment we have. On the day of the grand opening of the road, Grandpa and other dignitaries stood at the top of the pass while Grandpa cut the ribbon.

Of course, the highway to be made for our God cannot be and is not being built by *our* might or power. But glory to God, it's by the Spirit's might.

There is supernatural and divine equipment to help us do what we need to do in order for the glory of the Lord to be revealed. Through effective prayer we are building a highway that will give us access into particular places for the glory of God to be revealed.

Notice Isaiah 40:3–4 says that preparing a highway for God requires mountains to be removed. Jesus taught us in Mark 11:23–24 how to move mountains by speaking to them.

Mountain removal, however, is only part of highway building according to Isaiah 40:3. There is other work required as well if the road is to be finished.

Just as highway building takes time to complete in the natural, spiritual roads take time too. Road construction crews do as much as they can in any one day. The next day they pick up where they left off, and they keep at it from one day to the next until the road is finished and ready for use.

There is a ministry in prayer which is comparable to road building where diligence and persistence are required if the road is ever to be finished.

When we lived in Rome, the highways we traveled were built by the Roman Empire. The Roman Empire was the first to ever build highways. They knew the shortest distance between two points is a straight line and they set about very purposefully to build these highways.

In order to mobilize troops to the region they wanted to conquer, they would first build a road accessing that place. It took a lot of time and energy to make a highway, but in the long run it facilitated their plan. They also used those roads for communication and commerce.

The same principle is used in prayer. When Jesus wants to manifest His glory in a place for all to see, He needs a highway. Our voices, lifted in faith, are used not only as an avenue to receive blessings for our own selves but also to clear a way for the glory of Jesus to be revealed and ultimately for Him to come again.

You may ask, "How do we know when the road is finished?" Well, it's when the glory of the Lord is revealed in that particular destination and all the people there are able to see it!

God is the Master Planner. Before He manifests His presence in a place, He stirs a need in people's hearts to begin building a road to that place in prayer. He does this by planting a desire in our hearts, *His desire,* for His glory to be revealed to the people in a particular place.

So with a God-given passion, we start praying toward that destination, and every time we pray with His direction and power, progress is made. Just because we don't get to our destination when we say "amen" the first time doesn't mean we stop praying or get discouraged. No! Each time we pray effectively, we take and prepare more ground.

Sometimes high and exalted thinking is brought down during times of prayer. Sometimes low things, even people who don't think they can do anything or who are paralyzed by ignorance or intimidation, are brought up. Crooked things—things which aren't right—are straightened, and rough things are made smooth.

> Through effective prayer, we actually make the road on which the glory of God will travel.

We *keep* praying as the Holy Spirit directs us until the road reaches its destination, and the glory of the Lord is revealed in that place. Through effective prayer, we actually make the road on which the glory of God will travel.

While we are thrilled with testimonies of God's glory being manifested in cities, regions, and nations, we must bear in mind that those manifestations of God's glorious presence and power didn't

> The greater the glory, the greater the preparation.

"just happen." There was preparation. And the greater the glory, the greater the preparation. Without fail, each testimony of God's glory has had pioneer road teams that diligently and persistently prayed.

Over the years I've been a part of road teams that built roads to where the glory of the Lord was revealed. Road building for the manifestation of God's glory is one of the *greatest* privileges I have known in my life. The majority of road work is not done in front of the people it will affect. It is done only before God and for His glory!

We know generally that God wants to manifest His love and glory to all people and accomplish mighty works for them. But the roads to reach those people are not just general. If you want to go to a particular place, you must travel on a specific road. Not just "any old road" will get you there.

There are many different areas within nations to which God wants access. For instance, there's the business world, the legal and political arenas, and the educational sphere, just to name a few. There are specific roads which need to be built in specific areas by people who have been stirred by God with compassion to pray.

For example, there is a church Tony and I are closely connected to where the pastors were moved by compassion years ago to start praying for specific groups of people. They don't just pray for souls in general, but they target musicians, sports figures, people within the entertainment field, as well as specific nations. They have been diligent in prayer over the years to build the very roads which they themselves and others are now walking on in order to minister to the people they have prayed for.

While there is an important truth contained in Second Corinthians 6:17—"*Come out from among them And be separate, says the Lord. Do not touch what is unclean*"—it must be interpreted within a wider truth. We are not to love the world in the way that we *eat* of what it has to offer to satisfy our lives. It is impossible to eat of darkness and then bear fruit of light.

> *If we don't occupy . . . something else will!*

Darkness, however, is doomed to remain dark unless light is brought in. To evacuate the fields of education, politics, entertainment, and business because of the fear of defilement is to give the devil unhindered access to those areas for his purposes. If we don't occupy and put down roots, something else will (Luke 19:13, 2 Chron. chapter 28)!

One of the last things Jesus said for us to do was to GO into all the world and preach the Gospel to every creature (Mark 16:15). Jesus said, "*And this gospel of the kingdom will be preached in all the world as a witness to all the nations, and then the end will come*" (Matt. 24:14). Of course we want to see the glory manifested in our churches, but God wants the whole earth to be filled with the knowledge of His glory as the waters cover the sea (Hab. 2:14).

The Holy Spirit has been stirring the Church with the desire to access the places which are void of the glory of God. But desire alone will not get the job done.

John the Baptist prophesied as "one crying in the wilderness." He used his voice to bring mountains down and low places up. His voice straightened crooked things and smoothed out the rough places. Our voices, like John's, serve as a tool empowered by the Holy Spirit to prepare a road for Jesus and His ministry.

Just as the roles of people like Anna and Simeon will be reflected in the preparation for the Second Coming of Jesus, this ministry of John will also be mirrored in those who are involved in preparing the way of the Lord in these final days.

---

[1] *Strong's Exhaustive Concordance of the Bible*, G3598, *hodos*.

[2] *Strong's Exhaustive Concordance of the Bible*, H4546, *mecillah*.

CHAPTER 2

The Spirit and Power of Elijah

The life purpose of John the Baptist was to prepare the way for the First Coming of Jesus. He accomplished this in the *"spirit and power of Elijah"* (Luke 1:17). Jesus Himself actually called John by the name Elijah when He was on the Mount of Transfiguration.

MATTHEW 17:11–13

11 Jesus answered and said to them, "Indeed, Elijah is coming first and will restore all things.

12 But I say to you that Elijah has come already, and they did not know him but did to him whatever they wished. Likewise the Son of Man is also about to suffer at their hands."

13 Then the disciples understood that He spoke to them of John the Baptist.

So what is the *"spirit and power of Elijah"* in which John ministered? To better understand, we should go back and look at a couple of highlights in Elijah's ministry of restoration and preparation.

Prayer for Rain

In First Kings 18:1, three and a half years after Elijah declared there would be no rain, God tells him to show himself to King Ahab and that rain will come. Before the rain came, however, Elijah was used to restore the fear of the Lord in the house of Israel.

The people had become horribly confused about who they were. They had become so mixed up with the spirit of the world that there wasn't a clear delineation between God's people and the people of the world. The Holy Ghost worked through Elijah to separate Israel from the spirit of the world. That spirit had taken the form of Baal worship and had infiltrated the people of God.

Elijah challenged the people and said, *"If the Lord is God, follow Him"* (v. 21). He also confronted the prophets of Baal. He called down fire from Heaven and triumphed over those heathen prophets. God's people again proclaimed that Jehovah was indeed God after witnessing this demonstration of His almightiness (vv. 17–40).

At the end of this chapter, we see Elijah praying for the one thing God promised him at the beginning of the chapter—rain. God didn't promise him fire from Heaven or any other miracle. His only promise was rain. But rain was the only thing that didn't happen without persevering prayer!

So Elijah put his head between his knees and called on God. He sent his servant to see what was happening, but there was nothing happening. Six times this servant was sent, and six times he returned with a dreary report.

Isn't it interesting that there are some things God promises us which don't come to pass—at least not until we persevere in asking for them? Personally, I'm glad it didn't say, "He prayed and it rained," because as a pray-er, this account really helps me. He prayed and seemingly *nothing* happened! You can derive encouragement from this. I do!

Any promise of God needs someone to hold onto it. Prayer without a promise has no grounding, and there will be no fruit to your prayer. On the other hand, a promise without prayer has no purpose at all.

> Prayer without a promise has no grounding.

Promises are activated by believing prayer. Promises have been put in the Word for the purpose of holding fast to them. And prayer is one of the primary ways in which we do this. Promises are prayer tools. You never, ever let go of them. If God promised it, it will surely come to pass.

God gave Elijah a promise, and this man held onto that promise until he saw the answer. Even then, he didn't need a huge indication that the answer had come. A cloud the size of a man's hand was enough to cause him to outrun the king's chariot as he rushed to get in out of the rain!

James 5:7–8 uses the account of Elijah's prayer for rain to classically illustrate to us the kind of prayer which precedes and prepares the way for the coming of the Lord.

JAMES 5:7–8

7 Therefore be patient, brethren, until the COMING OF THE LORD. See how the farmer waits for the precious fruit of the earth, waiting patiently for it until it receives the early and latter rain.

8 You also be patient. Establish your hearts, for the COMING OF THE LORD is at hand.

Here James exhorts us to be patient for the coming of the Lord. An analogy can be drawn between this verse, with the patient husbandman waiting for the harvest, and God, the Lord of the harvest, waiting for a harvest of souls from all over the earth (Matt. 9:38).

The early and latter rains mentioned here are the spring and summer rains which bring the crops to ripeness. In the same way, the rain of God's Spirit falling on the field of human souls causes these souls to be ready for harvest. It is this harvest for which the coming of the Lord is patiently waiting.

A few verses later, Elijah's prayer for rain provides an excellent example of how to pray for the rain of God's Spirit:

JAMES 5:16–18 (Amplified)

16 The earnest (heartfelt, continued) prayer of a righteous man makes tremendous power available [dynamic in its working].

17 Elijah was a human being with a nature such as we have [with feelings, affections, and a constitution like ours]; and he prayed earnestly for it not to rain, and no rain fell on the earth for three years and six months. [1 Kings 17:1.]

18 And [then] he prayed again and the heavens supplied rain and the land produced its crops [as usual]. [1 Kings 18:42–45.]

Elijah was just as human as we are, and for three and a half years his prayers kept the rain from falling. But when he did finally pray fervently for rain, it fell from the skies and made the crops grow.

Let's see what the Bible has to say concerning the rain of God's Spirit. Here are some important aspects to consider:

- What is the rain? Hosea 6:3 says God comes as the rain. His very presence is the rain we are asking for.

- How does the rain fall? Like the dew, snow, or any other precipitation—with varying degrees of intensity. God's presence falls in different ways and measures.

- The rain falls over areas of the earth on both the just and the unjust (Matt. 5:45). It is God's presence alone which refreshes and revives the just (Acts 3:19) and prepares the unjust for harvesting (John 16:8–9).

- Although there was a promise for rain, Elijah had to pray, as we have just seen. Zechariah 10:1 says to ask for rain in the time of the latter rain. Do you see it? Even though we have a promise of an outpouring of God's Spirit, and even though it is the right time, we still have to ask.

- Elijah was persistent in his prayer for rain (Luke 18:1).

When fervent, persistent prayers are made for a specific harvest field such as the youth, business persons, specific nations, and the like, those prayers function the same way evaporation functions in bringing the rain. They will accumulate over that harvest field like a cloud. When that cloud reaches the point of saturation, it will turn into precipitation! The rain of God's presence will fall on that field and do just what James 5:18 says. It will cause it to be ready for harvest!

You can see why Elijah's example of praying for the rain is extremely important in preparing the way for Jesus' return. This rain is necessary to prepare the people of God as well as the harvest of souls for which He is patiently waiting.

Let us, as people who have been made righteous, pray earnest, heartfelt, and *continued* prayers, making tremendous power available, dynamic in its working. "Lord, send the rain!"

Elijah's Three Instructions From God

Elijah's experience on Mount Carmel was a spectacular display of God's power. The change which occurred in God's people was dramatic. However, with Jezebel still influencing the nation, Baal worship was far from over and done with. It would have to be uprooted. It was for this purpose that God called Elijah out of the cave and spoke in a still, small voice, instructing him to do three things. This would be God's last directive to Elijah the prophet, and it is from these instructions that we find insight into important factors in preparing the way of the Lord.

1 KINGS 19:15-17

15 Then the Lord said to him: "Go, return on your way to the Wilderness of Damascus; and when you arrive, anoint Hazael as king over Syria.

16 Also you shall anoint Jehu the son of Nimshi as king over Israel. And Elisha the son of Shaphat of Abel Meholah you shall anoint as prophet in your place.

17 It shall be that whoever escapes the sword of Hazael, Jehu will kill; and whoever escapes the sword of Jehu, Elisha will kill.

Elijah was instructed to do three things:

- Anoint Hazael to be king over Syria
- Anoint Jehu to be king over Israel
- Anoint Elisha to be a prophet in Elijah's place

Elisha—Prophet in Israel

Right away, Elijah found Elisha and put his mantle upon him (1 Kings 19:19). Elisha then faithfully served Elijah until

Elijah was taken up into Heaven. At the end of Elijah's life, Elisha followed him from place to place until they crossed the Jordan River, and a chariot of fire and horsemen took Elijah away. The only thing left was the mantle, which came floating down to the earth. That was the same mantle Elijah had cast on Elisha when he anointed him to take his place as prophet.

With that very mantle, Elisha struck the waters of the Jordan and the waters rolled back in the same way they had for Elijah, obviously with the same power and anointing. Elisha's request for a double portion of the anointing was granted, and twice as many miracles were recorded when he was prophet. Without a doubt, Elisha was anointed to be a prophet in Elijah's place (1 Kings 19:16).

> Of the three people God told Elijah to anoint, Elisha is the only one who is spoken of much.

Typically, of the three people God told Elijah to anoint, Elisha is the only one who is spoken of much. Many sermons have been preached about Elisha's faithfulness and commitment as an encouragement to those who desire an increase of God's anointing on their lives. The other two men are seldom mentioned and wouldn't be considered Bible characters who were anointed of God. Most of us would consider them to be unworthy candidates for the anointing.

Neither of them had been in the school of the prophets with Elijah. They weren't remotely godly. (Hazael wasn't even an Israelite!) But they must have been important to God's plan or He wouldn't have wasted the anointing on them. Why do I say that? The anointing enables people to do things for God which they wouldn't naturally be able to do. These two men had a portion of God's plan to fulfill and He anointed them to do it.

It is important to note here that Elijah personally anointed Elisha to be a prophet in his place. He didn't personally anoint Hazael or Jehu for their roles. How then was the directive to anoint these men carried out?

Hazael—Heathen King of Syria

What God had spoken concerning anointing Hazael to be king over Syria was carried out *after* Elijah left the earth. Hazael had to be anointed by someone who was actually anointed by God, and that man was Elisha. Elijah had anointed Elisha to be a prophet *by putting his mantle on him*, thereby qualifying Elisha to carry out God's directive. It was the anointing, not Elijah himself, which qualified Elisha to be a prophet.

Likewise, it was the anointing *through a prophetic word*, not Elijah personally, which qualified Hazael to be king of Syria. Elijah did the part he had to do personally when he anointed Elisha.

The account of Elisha's interaction with Hazael is a very interesting one. The king of Syria, Ben-Hadad, was sick. He told Hazael to go to Elisha and inquire of the Lord as to whether he would recover or not. So Hazael took some gifts and went to meet Elisha and asked him if the king would recover.

Elisha told Hazael to tell the king that he would recover, but he said to Hazael that the Lord had shown him the king would actually die of another cause! Elisha saw some other things too. As he stared at Hazael, Elisha began to weep. Take a look at what Elisha said:

2 KINGS 8:11-13 (Amplified)

11 Elisha stared steadily at him until Hazael was embarrassed. And the man of God wept.

12 And Hazael said, Why do you weep, my lord? He answered, Because I know the evil that you will do to the Israelites. You will burn their strongholds, slay their young men with the sword, dash their infants in pieces, and rip up their pregnant women.

13 And Hazael said, What is your servant, only a dog, that he should do this monstrous thing? And Elisha answered, The Lord has shown me that you will be king over Syria.

In Second Kings chapters 12 and 13, we see how Hazael, a heathen king, was used in the judgment of Israel brought on by their worship of Baal.

Jehu—Military Captain and King

Finally, Jehu, a military leader, is anointed and is the only one of the three on whom *anointing oil* is used. Elisha commissions one of the "sons of the prophets" to do the actual anointing. The Bible only identifies this prophet as a young man.

Remember, it is the anointing which enables people to fulfill their God-given purposes. Elisha told one of the sons of the prophets to take the flask of oil and look for Jehu, son of Jehoshaphat, son of Nimshi, take him into a room away from his brethren, and there anoint him as king over Israel. He was then instructed to open the door and run for his life!

The young man did as he was told. He spoke the word of the Lord over Jehu and prophesied what would take place.

2 KINGS 9:6-10

6 "Thus says the Lord God of Israel: 'I have anointed you king over the people of the Lord, over Israel.

7 You shall strike down the house of Ahab your master, that I may avenge the blood of My servants the prophets, and the blood of all the servants of the Lord, at the hand of Jezebel.

8 For the whole house of Ahab shall perish; and I will cut off from Ahab all the males in Israel, both bond and free.

9 So I will make the house of Ahab like the house of Jeroboam the son of Nebat, and like the house of Baasha the son of Ahijah.

10 The dogs shall eat Jezebel on the plot of ground at Jezreel,
and there shall be none to bury her.'" And he opened the
door and fled.

Jehu had a reputation for being a wild man, and he
accomplished his commission from the Lord brutally
(2 Kings chapters 9 and 10).

It would be good to mention here that the extreme measures used to purge the Israelites of this vile religion were not
simply an attack against Baal worship. We must remember
that the seed for the Redeemer of all mankind was being
protected.

From Abraham, God's covenant partner, came a family
which grew into the nation of Israel. Generations later, a family came from that nation, and from that family, Mary, the
mother of the world's Savior.

During Elisha's day, Israel was in danger of being entirely
taken over by Baal worship if it weren't completely driven
out. In order to achieve God's desire of eradicating this heathen religion from Israel, three people had to operate in three
separate areas of influence. If this goal could have been
accomplished through Elisha the prophet alone, God
wouldn't have anointed Hazael and Jehu.

No, God's plan was also to be carried out through Hazael,
a king—a heathen king, mind you! Finally, it was also to be
accomplished through Jehu, an experienced military leader.

The Transfer of Anointing

Remember, the last directive Elijah received from God involved the transfer of anointing. God wanted to drive out Baal worship from Israel in order to protect the line through which the Redeemer of the world would come. He gave Elijah instructions to bring the hearts of the people back to the Lord and prepare them for Himself.

God chose three individuals to carry out this directive and anointed all three to bring about His desired result. We saw how God passed the anointing from Elijah to Elisha, who then dispensed that anointing to Hazael as the king. Another prophet then dispensed it to Jehu, a military leader.

This shows us that the anointing, which is for God's purpose and plan, is transferred according to His direction and enables people to accomplish God-given assignments. Some of those assignments are carried out among the children of God, while others are fulfilled in a secular setting.

We would be mistaken to think that everything God has to do in preparation for Jesus' return could be done solely within the Church. God is not limited to working only inside the Church. Indeed, He is working in the Church and through the Church, but God is working in the nations as well. The

> God is not limited to working only inside the Church.

unfolding of His plan has a direct bearing on the rise and fall of leaders of nations and governments in these days and the days to come.

There are many accounts in the Bible where God gave kings directions for their nations. Likewise, military direction and strategy often came through prophets to achieve victory and execute judgments for the Lord.

In preparing the way for the Second Coming of the Lord, we are still seeing the anointing dispensed through the prophetic word and Spirit-led prayer. That anointing will certainly affect politicians as well as various people in many different levels and circles of authority.

Those who are anointed of God to accomplish particular tasks will not be exclusively those who stand in a pulpit. There will also be an anointing from God on political leaders as well as those in military and civil authority and other positions of influence.

> Don't be offended when you see the hand of God on someone you didn't expect Him to use.

As people of prayer, it is important that our panorama is widened so that when the Holy Spirit urges us to pray for people in these various positions, we don't discount and resist His direction because of wrong thinking. We cannot have minuscule thinking in these days, because the ways of the Lord are expansive. Don't be surprised about where you see the anointing, and don't be offended when you see the hand of God on someone you didn't expect Him to use. Be thrilled and certain that whenever you see the anointing, it is all working together to prepare the way of the Lord!

CHAPTER 3

Having Dominion in Your Garden

The Bible is full of promises and provisions which are to be appropriated for our personal lives. Consequently, the extent of many believers' prayer lives revolves around themselves and people who directly affect them, such as family and friends. However, there is a vast supply of power available for believers to pray effectively in a much larger arena.

Unless you are certain that you are authorized to pray in a broader circumference, which includes kings, presidents, and other people of authority and influence, you may never be bold enough to extend your prayers to those wider arenas. Your authorization and responsibility to pray for the kinds of people required to prepare the way of the Lord must be settled. To do that, we'll need to go back to the beginning—to God's direction to man when he was created.

GENESIS 1:27-28

27 So God created man in His own image; in the image of God He created him; male and female He created them.

28 Then God blessed them, and God said to them, "BE FRUITFUL AND MULTIPLY; FILL THE EARTH AND

SUBDUE IT; HAVE DOMINION over the fish of the sea, over the birds of the air, and over every living thing that moves on the earth."

> God created man to have dominion over the earth.

God created man to have dominion over the earth and over everything He had made in it. He also gave man the authority and the glory and power to do the job He had commanded him to do.

GENESIS 2:15

15 Then the Lord God took the man and put him in the garden of Eden to tend and keep it.

When God created man and crowned him with glory and honor and gave him dominion, He gave man a job. God did not intend for man to work in a toiling sense, but as a steward and keeper. He was put in the garden to guard it. But the extent of his dominion went beyond the garden; it included the whole earth.

If Adam and Even had used their dominion to tend the garden in which they were placed, the state of the garden would have grown and expanded. As Adam and Eve had children and multiplied, they would have all eventually filled and subdued the entire earth. The garden was the starting point of making the whole earth a garden: "Heaven on earth" under God-given dominion.

PSALM 115:16

16 The heaven, even the heavens, are the Lord's; But the earth
He has given to the children of men.

Psalm 115:16 says that Heaven belongs to God, which
explains exactly why Heaven is a wonderful place. Heaven is
the place where there is a complete absence of anything bad.
There is no crime there, no hurting, no suffering, no war, no
murder, no lying, or stealing. There is *nothing* bad there. That
is what makes Heaven "heavenly"!

We could say Heaven is the way it is because in Heaven
God always gets His way. In Heaven no one tells God "NO!"
Actually, some time ago someone did tell God "No," and he's
not there anymore. Those who sided with him left with him
as well. Ever since Lucifer left Heaven, God has always gotten
His way.

Psalm 115:16 goes on to say that God has given the earth
to the children of men, which also explains many things. The
earth is in the condition it's in because it belongs to man.

Crime, suffering, war, and pov-
erty are not the way God intended
for things to be on the earth. It certainly is not the way He created it,
nor was it in that state when he delegated it to man. How did it get in
the shape it is now? The dominion
that God gave man was not just a
blessing: dominion is a vocation.

> The dominion that
> God gave man was
> not just a blessing:
> dominion is a
> vocation.

The *Webster's Revised Unabridged Dictionary (1913)* definition for *dominion* is "sovereign or supreme authority; the power of governing and controlling; sovereignty; supremacy."[1]

Let's consider the office of the president of the United States, a position which holds great honor all over the world. The president can visit countries that don't even like him and they are still nice to him! They play music for him and give him the best room and the best food. They give him preferential treatment.

But if the president, having this wonderful place of honor, just hung out at a resort, ate pretzels, played golf, and only *watched* the news from a recliner, he would not be a good president. If he were waiting for the next banquet just so he could wear a new suit and tie and enjoy all the fuss and fanfare, but in between all the banquets and ceremonies he just wanted to relax and have a good time, what would we think of such a person?

Although the American people are glad for the president to be honored wherever he goes, they also expect him to *work*! In fact, if he didn't work, he would not be tolerated. His position is indeed one of great honor, but it is also a position of *responsibility*!

Adam held that kind of position of responsibility in the garden. What went wrong? Genesis 1:28 says God commanded Adam to be fruitful, multiply, and replenish the earth. He also gave Adam a second commandment, which was to have dominion and subdue the earth and everything in it. There was a third commandment in Genesis 2:17, which was to not eat of the tree of the knowledge of good and evil.

When we remember the sins Adam committed, what do we think of? We always think about the fact that he partook of the fruit of the tree of the knowledge of good and evil. But that was actually not his first mistake.

The first thing Adam did wrong was not a sin of *commission* but a sin of *omission*. He never would have had the problem of eating of the fruit if he had taken dominion over the serpent when he came into the garden to tempt Eve. Don't you wish he had done that?

If Adam had obeyed the second command God gave him, he would have said to the serpent, "Get out of my garden and don't ever come back here again! And leave my wife alone!" But that is not the way it happened. The Bible says Eve was deceived but Adam was not. He lost his job because he didn't show up for it. He disregarded God's second command to him.

Because he didn't dominate the serpent, the god of this world, whom he was originally given dominion over, he became dominated. But praise be to God, in Jesus' work of redemption, Jesus got our job—our dominion—back! (More on this in the following chapter.)

> Jesus, as the second Adam, undid everything the first Adam had done.

The work of redemption was not just to give us a better life; it was to give us *His* life. Jesus, as the second Adam, undid everything the first Adam had done. The first Adam was not responsible with the job he had been given. However, the Second Adam, Jesus, was responsible to the Father His entire life and did exactly what God told Him to do (Heb. 3:2–6).

We are *in* that Second Adam, Jesus, so we have been given authority to reign in this life through Him (Rom. 5:17). Originally, the first Adam had dominion over the earth. Now, as a result of our being born again, dominion has been restored to us.

We have seen in Genesis 2:15 that God did not tell Adam to have dominion merely over himself, but He delegated to him dominion over *everything* that was on the earth. Today, with dominion restored to us, it is very important for us to be aware of everything that is in our garden, because it represents our jurisdiction.

We cannot command authority outside of our jurisdiction, but we are responsible for what is within its parameters. In other words, we are responsible for what is in our "garden." If we don't know what is in our "garden," are we excused from the responsibility of guarding what is in it?

Look at it this way. What if you were pulled over by a police officer for speeding and he said you were going well over the speed limit? Would it make a difference for you to plead ignorance and tell him you did not see the sign? Do you think he would excuse you, apologize for taking your time, and send you on your way? NO! Just because you didn't see the sign doesn't remove the responsibility from you! Even if you didn't see it, you are still responsible!

So it is with the jurisdiction we have been given by God. We are responsible for what is in our garden even if we don't know it. The devil hopes we never find out what is in our garden because if we fail to exercise our authority, then we lose territory by default. This is a spiritual principle. This is what happened in the beginning with Adam.

First of all, the devil hopes you don't find out that you do have authority. Second, if you know you have authority and dominion, he just hopes you won't use it. Having authority but not using it will yield the same results as not having any authority at all. The devil will be able to take territory from you regardless.

You not only have a *right* in Christ, but you also have a *responsibility* to simply say "No!" when the devil tries to attack you in any way! If the devil tries to come against your finances, you have a right and a responsibility to say, "No!" If he tries to break up your family or destroy your life, you have a right and a responsibility to say, "No!"

There is a responsibility to keep ourselves and we have been given the dominion and authority to do just that. The Bible tells us that we are to:

- Keep our hearts with all diligence (Prov. 4:23)

- Keep ourselves pure (1 Tim. 5:22)

- Keep ourselves unspotted from the world (James 1:27)

- Keep ourselves from idols (1 John 5:21)

- Keep guard over our thought life (2 Cor. 10:5, Phil. 4:6)

- Keep ourselves in the love of God (Jude 21)

Our dominion, however, goes beyond the parameters of our own person. Genesis 2:15 says that God put Adam in a garden and gave him dominion. But his jurisdiction was broader than just his own body; he had dominion over everything in the garden.

> **What else is in your garden?**

What about your "garden"? What else is in your garden besides you? Anything God said to pray about in His Word would be in your garden. That's why it is so important to know what the Bible says to pray about. The Bible gives us instruction about how and what to pray for ourselves and for one another.

Other people in the Body of Christ are in our garden. We are to guard and watch over each other. We are to pray for one another, carry each others' burdens and so fulfill the law of Christ (Gal. 6:2, Eph. 6:18).

Jesus instructed us to even pray for our enemies (Matt. 5:44). Many times unkind or wicked people will be in our garden! Within that instruction, God has given us not only the right but the responsibility to pray for those who are our enemies.

Divine Strategy for All Men to Be Saved

An outlined directive to pray for all men is given to us in First Timothy 2:1-4. Therefore, all men are included in our garden as part of our responsibility for prayer.

1 TIMOTHY 2:1-4

1 Therefore I exhort first of all that supplications, prayers, intercessions, and giving of thanks be made for all men,

2 for kings and all who are in authority, that we may lead a quiet and peaceable life in all godliness and reverence.

3 For this is good and acceptable in the sight of God our Savior,

4 who desires all men to be saved and to come to the knowledge of the truth.

Paul's urgent instruction to his spiritual son, Timothy, listed various kinds of prayers to be made for *all men.*

If the first thing this passage tells us to do is pray for all men, it is right for us to pray for all men. It would not be correct for us to look around and think that our family and dear friends are the only ones with us in our garden. Because the Bible says to pray for all men, God makes it possible by the Holy Spirit's help for us to pray for all men. Praying for the rain of God's presence, as discussed in the previous chapter, is one effective way to pray for all men.

> We are to pray for "kings and all who are in authority."

Secondly, it says we are to pray for "*kings and all who are in authority.*" By telling us to pray for these people, we are authorized to do so.

I had the privilege of assisting Brother Kenneth E. Hagin start Prayer and Healing School on the RHEMA campus in 1979. There were three primary reasons Brother Hagin felt compelled to have a school of prayer:

- For the people attending Healing School
- For teaching and demonstrating the principles of prayer
- For the purpose of praying for kings and all in authority

First Timothy 2:1–4 was a foundational scripture and was used regularly to direct the subject of prayer. There was no one more indifferent and unconcerned than I was about this particular subject of prayer. I fervently prayed about the spreading of the Gospel to all men and a move of God's Spirit in our services but cooled off quickly on the subject of kings and all those in authority. To me, it was boring and unrelated to important matters such as people being saved.

When I eventually came to lead Prayer School, it was my responsibility to carry on prayer for this subject. Oh, how difficult it was for me, until it seemed that I began to pick up the pulse of God's heart through this amazing scripture. When this passage came alive to me, it unfolded in my heart, and I saw a divine strategy within these verses.

Notice that in verse one we are instructed to pray for *all* men. And verse four explains why, stating that God wants *all* men to be saved and come to the knowledge of the truth. He paid the price by the blood of His own Son for *all* men to be saved. If our desire, however, is for just a family member or a few friends to come into our church, then the strategy placed in this scripture may be overlooked. It may be obeyed and performed dutifully, as I did, but it will not be done from the heart.

The Lord showed me that if I shared His desire for all men to be saved and come to the knowledge of the truth, I would need to be aware of and embrace the instruction sandwiched between verses one and four. With this in mind, you can see that by targeting kings and people in positions of authority, the "all men" under the influence of those persons will be affected. You can actually affect more people in prayer when you pray for those in authority over them.

Along with this urgent exhortation to pray for "*kings and all who are in authority*" comes the authorization for us to pray for these people. Note that the term "kings" is plural, indicating that we should pray for kings other than our own, as well as any and all persons of authority and influence. It is glorious to think that people of outstanding influence, whom you see on televisions and in magazines, can actually be influenced by what the Holy Spirit inspires *you* to pray!

Look around your "garden." In addition to yourself, your family, and friends, First Timothy 2:1–2 mentions others you have been instructed to pray for. Therefore, you have a right and responsibility to pray for all those mentioned. Let's pray, knowing that the Holy Spirit, who is our Helper, cannot help us if we're doing nothing. But He is ever ready to inspire and empower us when we pray in this arena.

---

[1] *Webster's Revised Unabridged Dictionary*, 1913 ed., s.v. "dominion," http://machaut.uchicago.edu/cgi-bin/WEBSTER.sh?WORD= DOMINION.

CHAPTER 4

Platforms in Prayer

Every child of God has a right to fellowship with the Father. Every believer has a right to pray. Not only do we have a right, but we have seen in the previous chapter that we have a responsibility to pray for the things which God commissions us to pray for. You may be familiar with the authority given to us by Jesus Christ and may even be applying this in your own personal life. But when it comes to praying for people of influence, have you ever felt inadequate?

What qualifies *you* to be used of God to dispense anointing to a president or someone else of authority? How can you, an individual citizen, pray for your nation's leader? Does anything really happen when you pray for your nation or any nation?

Not having a clear understanding of the answers to these questions may intimidate you and stop you from praying in this particular arena. How you view God *and* yourself in relation to situations and people you are praying for will change the way you pray and alter the results of your prayers.

There are three different platforms, or points of view, from which prayer is commonly presented.

Platform One

presidents, people of authority and influence, nations: great and small, movie stars, Jesus, angels, demons, educators, doctors, the Bible, lawyers, sports figures

Did you locate Jesus somewhere in the list on the left? Should He and the will of His Kingdom even be on a list amidst those other names?

A person who prays from Platform One sees himself as a powerless individual with little, if any, hope for supernatural intervention. He does not see God, if He exists, as a ruler or as more powerful than the situation. Prayer from this platform, if it is made at all, is most of the time ineffectual.

> A person who prays from Platform One sees himself as a powerless individual with little, if any, hope for supernatural intervention.

People with this perception of reality rarely pray, because it is pointless. The situation is just too overwhelming for them to even try to pray, and if they do, it's sometimes no more than a "shot in the dark."

A prayer from this position may sound like, "God, if You really do exist and are real, *do something!*" Yet, there are glorious testimonies of God's merciful intervention in answer to these desperate prayers.

Platform Two

A person who prays from Platform Two acknowledges God as being above all circumstances and situations, but his prayer is motivated by circumstances and situations rather than a prompting of the Holy Spirit.

On Platform Two, the pray-er sees God as being above all other names. However, if the pray-er sees himself as below the situation and the persons for whom he is praying, his prayer from this platform may take on a tone of begging and pleading for God to do something.

In Second Chronicles chapter 20, this platform was established before effective prayer was made. In this account, the people of Israel began their prayer by worshiping God as the Creator and the One over the nations, before they presented their request for help against enemy nations who were much stronger than they. A similar example is found in Acts chapter 3. When the threat from religious leaders looked insurmountable, the apostles magnified God until His place *in their own consciousness* was not below or even in the middle of the situation, but above it.

These and other Biblical examples of prayer during a time of national crisis and disaster show how people prayed from this position. Even people who don't normally pray, can and do pray from this position in times of crisis. And God delivers them when people call out to Him (Joel 2:32, Acts 2:21).

Platform Three

God

presidents, people of authority and influence, nations: great and small, movie stars, angels, demons, educators, doctors, lawyers, sports figures

Platform Three is the position from which God intended prayer to take place on a consistent basis. This is the platform where we are seated with Christ in heavenly places at the right hand of God. The pray-er uses this high place in Christ to work together with God, not just in times of crisis or disaster, but continually, so that the will of God can be accomplished on earth. Not only is Christ above anything or anyone being prayed for, but the pray-er is in Him, above every name.

From this platform the pray-er's primary motivation to pray is by the unction of the Holy Spirit, not according to the pressures and demands of a crisis.

> The pray-er's primary motivation to pray is by the unction of the Holy Spirit.

From this platform the pray-er can see things from God's perspective and gain a wide panorama of the plan of God.

From this platform the pray-er is not hearing news; he is making news!

You can only pray from the platform of truth on which you stand. Natural status, name, wealth, fame, and political or business position have absolutely no bearing on which platform you pray from. The more enlightenment you have regarding your position in Christ Jesus, the higher the platform of prayer from which you will pray. And the higher the platform of prayer, the more effective and far-reaching your prayer will be.

The Greek philosopher and physicist Archimedes once said, "Give me a place to stand and I will move the earth." He understood the physical principle of the lever. Using this principle makes it possible to move an enormously heavy load with a small amount of physical exertion. However, it is only possible provided you have a lever that is rigid enough and you are at a sufficient distance from the load to be moved.

Archimedes With Lever[1]

This also illustrates a dynamic spiritual principle. In prayer, huge obstacles can be moved if we know the right place to stand—in a place far above the load and using a lever that is unbending and sturdy. There is no higher place from which to pray than the Throne of God. There is no stronger force to move situations than the Word of God. The completed work of Jesus Christ gives us the authority as well as the position to speak inspired words that will move mountains and affect the world.

---

[1] The engraving is from *Mechanic's Magazine* (cover of bound Volume II, Knight & Lacey, London, 1824). Courtesy of the *Annenberg Rare Book & Manuscript Library*, University of Pennsylvania, Philadelphia, USA. http://www.math.nyu.edu/~crorres/Archimedes/Lever/LeverIntro.html.

CHAPTER 5

Enforcing the Triumph of Christ

In the first chapter of Ephesians, Paul is praying for the church in Ephesus. Verse 19 makes a specific request for believers in this church to have a revelation of the exceeding greatness of God's power toward them.

EPHESIANS 1:16–23

16 [I] do not cease to give thanks for you, making mention of you in my prayers:

17 that the God of our Lord Jesus Christ, the Father of glory, may give to you the spirit of wisdom and revelation in the knowledge of Him,

18 the eyes of your understanding being enlightened; that you may know what is the hope of His calling, what are the riches of the glory of His inheritance in the saints,

19 and what is the exceeding greatness of His power toward us who believe, according to the working of His mighty power

20 which He worked in Christ when He raised Him from the dead and seated Him at His right hand in the heavenly places,

21 far above all principality and power and might and dominion, and every name that is named, not only in this age but also in that which is to come.

22 And He put all things under His feet, and gave Him to be head over all things to the church,

23 which is His body, the fullness of Him who fills all in all.

Every believer, everywhere, has a right to know the same truth of their dominion in Christ.

Even though this prayer was prayed specifically for the church at Ephesus, it was inspired by the Holy Spirit and therefore is an appropriate prayer for every believer and every church in any nation of the world. Every believer, everywhere, has a right to know the same truth of their dominion in Christ.

Every person in every rank of authority and importance is far below the Name and position given the Lord Jesus.

The power for which the Holy Spirit inspired Paul to request understanding is the same power which actually raised Jesus from the dead. This resurrection power not only brought Jesus back to life, but continued to raise Him until He was seated far above all principality, power, might, dominion, and every name which is named. Without a doubt, every person in every rank of authority and importance is far below the Name and position given the Lord Jesus (Phil. 2:9–10).

If the revelation of what Paul asked for was automatically known by all Christians, there wouldn't have been a need for this prayer. The prayer would have been nonessential. Instead, Paul said he never ceased to pray this prayer for the Ephesians.

A Position of Authority

An effective pray-er must recognize the fact that Jesus died, was buried, raised, and has been seated far above any demon spirit or principality that will be encountered or name that will be mentioned in the time of prayer. A consciousness of Jesus' supreme position establishes what was illustrated in Platform Two. But let's not stop there! Notice what is written: "*. . . and RAISED US UP TOGETHER, and made us SIT TOGETHER in the heavenly places in Christ Jesus . . .*" (Eph. 2:6).

After the Holy Spirit reveals truth to us, we then have a choice. Will we only privately enjoy the blessing and freedom which acting on it brings, or will we realize the truth is our weaponry which we use to help others be free also?

If you are only praying for yourself and your own personal benefits, you may not require the enormous revelation which this scripture invites. If you are only using your authority over demons that may come against you personally, such a revelation of the grand exaltation that we have in Christ may seem extreme.

However, if you are going to pray for governments and kings, or for cities and nations, it is imperative that you comprehend the benefits of implementing this prayer. The highest and most effective place from which to pray for all men, kings, and people of authority and influence, is the revelation that *I have been exalted with Him.*

> Jesus didn't come to the earth to pursue a private victorious life.

Jesus didn't come to the earth to pursue a private victorious life. He didn't look on humanity and say, "I have life and life more abundantly. It's a shame that you don't." No, He came to *give* life, not just receive and enjoy it. Jesus died so that our lives could be victorious and glorify the Father.

As God's sons and daughters, we are destined to look and act just like the First Born (Rom. 8:29). We have a responsibility before God the Father to declare and enforce the victory Jesus died to give us. To do that, we are going to *need* the revelation and understanding for which this prayer in Ephesians asks.

If I pray without a consciousness of my position in Christ Jesus, I pray as a mere human being instead of the child of God that I am. I cannot truly honor the price Jesus paid to regain man's dominion without actually walking in that dominion. Knowing the authority which belongs to the believer is essential to effective prayer and in preparing the way of the King of Kings.

Only to the degree to which I pray in the light of the triumph of Christ can I enforce that triumph. Empowered by that truth, I am no longer tentative, but filled with boldness. Revelation of my triumph with Christ takes the whine out of my voice. It takes all hesitancy away from me, and it puts a scepter in my hand.

> Only to the degree
> to which I pray
> in the light of
> the triumph
> of Christ
> can I enforce
> that triumph.

Nothing will give us "muscle" in prayer like feeding on scriptures regarding the work Jesus did for us and our identification with Him. Powerful prayer is not determined by the volume of our voice, but by our spiritual position—a position of strength.

ROMANS 5:17 (CEV)

17 Death ruled like a king because Adam had sinned. But that cannot compare with what Jesus Christ has done. God has been so kind to us, and he has accepted us because of Jesus. And so we will live and rule like kings.

The work Jesus accomplished in His death and resurrection gave us a tremendous gift of righteousness. According to Proverbs 28:1, the wicked flee when no one is even pursuing, but the righteous man is as bold as a lion. Our receiving abundant grace and the gift of righteousness makes all the difference. It determines whether death reigns in our lives, or we boldly reign. What a glorious right! What an awesome responsibility!

> We are to take His victory and enforce it in our lives and in the earth.

We are to take His victory and enforce it in our lives and in the earth in any way the Holy Ghost may direct.

The Rod of God

This Old Testament story superbly illustrates what happens with the use of our authority in Jesus. Amalek came out to fight with Israel while Moses stood on top of the hill with the rod of God in his hand.

EXODUS 17:8-11

8 Now Amalek came and fought with Israel in Rephidim.

9 And Moses said to Joshua, "Choose us some men and go out, fight with Amalek. Tomorrow I will stand ON THE TOP OF THE HILL WITH THE ROD OF GOD IN MY HAND."

10 So Joshua did as Moses said to him, and fought with Amalek. And Moses, Aaron, and Hur went up to the top of the hill.

11 And so it was, WHEN MOSES HELD UP HIS HAND, THAT ISRAEL PREVAILED; AND WHEN HE LET DOWN HIS HAND, AMALEK PREVAILED.

Notice that the children of God prevailed only when Moses' hands held up the rod. When he let down his hands, the enemy prevailed.

Now it doesn't say that Moses came down off the hill or even that he dropped the rod. All that was needed for the enemy to prevail was simply that the rod in Moses' hands was not lifted up.

This is a wonderful picture of our joint seating in Christ, *far* above principalities, powers, any dominion or kingdom, and every name which is named.

The Message Bible describes Jesus' seating this way: *"All this energy issues from Christ: God raised him from death and set him on a throne in deep heaven, in charge of running the universe, everything from galaxies to governments, no name and no power exempt from his rule. And not just for the time being, but forever"* (Eph. 1:20–21).

There are many wonderful analogies which can be derived from this story, but for the subject we are discussing, the rod beautifully symbolizes the authority of God delegated to man. You can see the use of the rod in Moses' life in the time of the plagues, the parting of the Red Sea, and bringing water out of a rock. It demonstrated God's authority in the hand of Moses.

The parallels are very obvious. Jesus did the work required to put us up on the hill. We could never have gotten to that place of dominion by ourselves. *He* raised us up and seated us in Christ Jesus, at the right hand of His throne. To be seated with Christ in this place of authority took an amazing display of the mighty power of God. It took *"the exceeding greatness of His power"* (Eph. 1:19).

Nonetheless, our joint seating alone does not secure victory against the opposing forces of darkness in this world. It is exercising and *maintaining the use of that authority* which drives back the enemy and secures our victory in this natural world.

With only *sporadic* use of our authority, there is little wonder why, little by little, the forces of darkness have invaded our schools, our government, and our society. How does a spirit of antichrist gain prevalence in any nation? How and when does this happen? It never happens "all of a sudden," but little by little as believers get tired of keeping their authority up or begin to think that responsibility lies only within a few certain Christians.

> Jesus restored us to a seat of authority and placed the rod of dominion in our hands.

Jesus restored us to a seat of authority and placed the rod of dominion in our hands. This rod is now ours to raise! How, exactly, do we raise it? We raise it through what we pray, what we declare, and even what we do. The use of our authority should not be limited to a prayer session once a week or even once a day. It should become a normal part of our lives as we become more and more conscious of the fact that we are in Christ and He, the victorious One, is in us!

> The use of our authority should not be limited to a prayer session once a week or even once a day.

The measure we raise our rod of dominion is the measure of God's purpose that will prevail on the earth. Let us help and encourage one another to walk with more than a part-time consciousness of the triumph of Christ and our dominion in Him. A persistent use of our authority is what the Holy Spirit is inspiring in these days of preparation before Jesus returns.

CHAPTER 6

Three Kinds of Kings

The Apostle Paul writes in Timothy that we are to pray for kings. The light of the Word in this particular arena will enable us to better incorporate the Holy Spirit's directions in prayer.

1 TIMOTHY 2:1-2 (Amplified)

1 First of all, then, I admonish and urge that petitions, prayers, intercessions, and thanksgivings be offered . . .

2 FOR KINGS . . .

When prayer is made for different nations of the world, it becomes apparent that there are different kinds of kings, presidents, or prime ministers. Some are Christians, others are at least upright and just, and still others are totally wicked. The Bible gives great examples of God utilizing these three kinds of kings for His plans, and that will help us as we pray for them.

The 'David' Kind of King

ACTS 13:22, 36 (Amplified)

22 And when He had deposed him [Saul], He raised up David to be their king; of him He bore witness and said, I have

found David son of Jesse A MAN AFTER MY OWN HEART, WHO WILL DO ALL MY WILL AND CARRY OUT MY PROGRAM FULLY.

36 For David, after he had SERVED GOD'S WILL AND PURPOSE AND COUNSEL in his own generation, fell asleep [in death] and was buried among his forefathers.

> David followed God with his whole heart and completely fulfilled the plan of God for his life.

David followed God with his whole heart and completely fulfilled the plan of God for his life. This did not occur by accident.

I have, on occasion, accidentally done the will of the Lord and found myself in the right place thinking, "How did I ever get here?" How wonderful it is when God guides you to the right place at the right time and you weren't even aware of it! As wonderful and good as this is, you cannot live your whole life this way. The Bible teaches us to purposefully seek the Lord with our whole heart. This is what David did.

David followed after God's heart consciously and he fulfilled God's plan for his life completely. He is an example for us today of a Christian king.

When we pray for the kings of nations, there are times when we get to pray for the "David" kind of king. They may seem rare, but they do exist!

David was not a perfect man and actually made some ghastly mistakes. But even though he made mistakes, he humbled himself. He didn't defend himself nor did he cast blame on others, and this was pleasing to God.

There are Christian leaders in government who are like David in this regard. Their hearts' desire is to do right and if they make mistakes, they are unintentional. It is a pleasure to pray for this kind of person. This, however, is not the only kind of king we will pray about.

First Timothy 2:2 instructs us not to merely pray for Christian kings and those who lead godly nations, like Israel's King David. God wants us to literally follow His Word and pray for *all* kings, regardless of what nation they rule and whether or not they are Christians.

The 'Cyrus' Kind of King

ISAIAH 44:28 (Amplified)

28 Who says of Cyrus, He is My shepherd (ruler), and he shall perform all My pleasure and fulfill all My purpose—even saying of Jerusalem, She shall [again] be built, and of the temple, Your foundation shall [again] be laid.

ISAIAH 45:1-3 (Amplified)

1 Thus says the Lord to HIS ANOINTED, TO CYRUS, whose right hand I have held to subdue nations before him, and I will unarm and ungird the loins of kings to open doors before him, so that gates will not be shut.

2 I will go before you and level the mountains [to make the crooked places straight]; I will break in pieces the doors of bronze and cut asunder the bars of iron.

3 And I will give you the treasures of darkness and hidden riches of secret places, that you may know that it is I, the Lord, the God of Israel, Who calls you by your name.

God calls Cyrus "His anointed." We are well acquainted with the fact that prophets are anointed and Israel's kings were anointed, but this man was not Israel's king. He was, nevertheless, anointed by God and given this assignment in fulfillment of prophecy.

EZRA 1:1–3 (Amplified)

1 Now in the first year of Cyrus king of Persia [almost seventy years after the first Jewish captives were taken to Babylon], that the word of the Lord by the mouth of Jeremiah might begin to be accomplished, THE LORD STIRRED UP THE SPIRIT OF CYRUS KING OF PERSIA so that he made a proclamation throughout all his kingdom and put it also in writing:

2 Thus says Cyrus king of Persia: The Lord, the God of Heaven, has given me all the kingdoms of the earth, and He has charged me to build Him a house at Jerusalem in Judah.

3 Whoever is among you of all His people, may his God be with him, and let him go up to Jerusalem in Judah and rebuild the house of the Lord, the God of Israel, in Jerusalem; He is God.

Further in this passage, Cyrus commissioned animals to be given and the people of God were granted safe passage. He also gave vast riches to enable this work of the Lord to be accomplished (Ezra chapter 7).

It would be typical to think that when prophecies are fulfilled, they will be fulfilled by people who are seeking God and praying. Sometimes this is the case, but not every time.

Cyrus, for example, was king of a pagan nation, but God anointed him to do what no one else had the authority or the wealth to do! Only Cyrus could commission the Jews, who were subject to him, to go home to Jerusalem and rebuild the temple.

> *Cyrus, for example, was king of a pagan nation, but God anointed him to do what no one else had the authority or the wealth to do!*

God anointed him and moved on him to make a decree and Cyrus did it! This is a most amazing thing. God has moved on people in churches and gotten little and sometimes no response, but He moved on this Persian king and got his full participation.

Cyrus' kindness toward the Jews was surely not passed down from his parents. Cyrus was the king of the Medes and Persians and was the son of Cambyses the Persian, and of Mandane, daughter of Astyages, king of the Medes. Both his father and grandfather had a blatant disregard for human life and were known for their barbarous treatment of people.

What was it that caused Cyrus to be so usable in God's divine plan? Some historians refer to Zoroaster, a Persian prophet whose teachings of kindness and good against evil could have influenced Cyrus' life. However, we do know for certain that 210 years before Cyrus was born, Isaiah prophesied about him by name (Isa. 44:28). Furthermore, Josephus the Jewish historian said that Cyrus read this prophecy concerning himself. As an actor follows his lines in a script, Cyrus "acted out" precisely what God said he would do, even though it was against normal policy.

> Spirit-directed praying invokes divine intervention and influences so that this kind of king will respond when God stirs his heart with His assignments.

Could God use a non-Jewish king of a pagan nation to fulfill His plan for His own people? Obviously He did! And with this precedent, we can be sure He has and will use a "Cyrus" type of king as required. Spirit-directed praying invokes divine intervention and influences so that this kind of king will respond when God stirs his heart with His assignments.

In 1985, after years of believers praying consistently and earnestly for the Gospel to have free access into communist countries in the former Eastern Bloc nations, the answer came through Mikhail Gorbachev. You know, he didn't do everything right. In fact, he had some very "un-Christian" ideas. But from his position of authority as president of the former Soviet Union, he presented the extremely radical idea of "Glasnost."

No one else thought he could pull it off, but President Gorbachev was anointed to succeed. People who rose up against him couldn't stand and those who encouraged him, such as Ronald Reagan and Pope John Paul II, were divinely strengthened. Mr. Gorbachev was anointed and favored by God to completely change a political system without bloodshed while the world just stood by and watched. All the prophets in the world couldn't have done it nor could all the mightiest preachers put together, unless they were anointed to do so as was President Gorbachev.

While Christians prayed Spirit-directed prayers as a part of dispensing the anointing, it was actually a leader in a position of authority whom God used to change the government. In order for the will of God to be done and for the Gospel to have access into that country, a road had to be opened which hadn't existed previously. God anointed and used a president in the making of that particular highway, and in doing so, fulfilled prophecies about that country.

There are other leaders today who are not Christians, but with God's anointing on them, they will fit nicely into His plan. The point is that we don't pray for kings because they are Christians, but because they are *kings*, and *God* says to pray for kings.

When Paul wrote this instruction to Timothy, he was in a prison in Rome. The Emperor Nero's selfishness and wickedness had sparked a persecution against the Christians. Look in any of Paul's letters, five of which were written from prison, and you will not find one complaint against Nero. Not one. Writing very little concerning the natural government of his time causes the few verses Paul does write on the subject to SHOUT! He says to pray for kings. That would mean it is absolutely right to pray for all kings, which enables God to intervene and further His divine plans.

The 'Pharaoh' Kind of King

> The Holy Spirit may direct us to pray for a third type of king who may seem totally unusable but also fits into God's master plan.

In preparing the way of the Lord, the Holy Spirit may direct us to pray for a third type of king who may seem totally unusable but also fits into God's master plan.

ROMANS 9:17 (Amplified)

17 For the Scripture says to Pharaoh, I HAVE RAISED YOU UP for this very purpose of displaying My power in [dealing with] you, so that My name may be proclaimed the whole world over.

Pharaoh was a wicked king and an enemy to God's people but the Word says that *God* raised him up. He employed

Pharaoh to demonstrate His power. We may think that we need to pray *against* these types of kings. There is no indication in the New Testament that we should pray against *any* kings. If we pray *for* them, God does interesting things with our prayers.

In the case of Pharaoh, we see in the Scripture that in between some of the plagues, God "hardened his heart" (Exod. 10:1). Sometimes it says that Pharaoh hardened his own heart (Exod. 8:15, 32). You see, the things that happened during the plagues would have softened a humble and repentant heart. But those plagues and God's dealings in Egypt hardened Pharaoh's heart.

There is an old saying that goes, "The same sun that softens wax, hardens clay."

> "The same sun that softens wax, hardens clay."

Those plagues would have made a "David" or "Cyrus" kind of king repent in sackcloth and ashes. However, Pharaoh's heart was not the same as David's or Cyrus'. Every time a plague was brought, instead of softening his heart, it became more hardened. Even so, Pharaoh actually accomplished a great purpose in the plan of God. He kicked the children of Israel out of Egypt in only a few days' time. This hardening process had the effect of speeding things up. In addition, the reports of the 10 plagues preceded the children of Israel to the Promised Land, making their enemies afraid of them.

It is very important when God gives you something to pray about that you don't draw back because it doesn't fit in your mind. This kind of king needs our prayers just as much as any other kind, and our prayers have great effect in bringing God's plan into being.

Let's look at another example of how God can use this "Pharaoh" type of king in carrying out His plan and purpose in the earth.

ACTS 4:26–30 (Amplified)

26 The kings of the earth took their stand in array [for attack] and the rulers were assembled and combined together against the Lord and against His Anointed (Christ, the Messiah).

27 For in this city there actually met and plotted together against Your holy Child and Servant Jesus, Whom YOU CONSECRATED BY ANOINTING, BOTH HEROD AND PONTIUS PILATE WITH THE GENTILES AND PEOPLES OF ISRAEL,

28 TO CARRY OUT ALL THAT YOUR HAND AND YOUR WILL AND PURPOSE HAD PREDESTINED (PREDE-TERMINED) SHOULD OCCUR.

29 And now, Lord, observe their threats and grant to Your bond servants [full freedom] to declare Your message fearlessly,

30 While You stretch out Your hand to cure and to perform signs and wonders through the authority and by the power of the name of Your holy Child and Servant Jesus.

Look closely at verse 27. It says that Herod, Pontius Pilate, the Gentiles, and the people of Israel came together. And why? Verse 28 tells us. It was to carry out all that *GOD'S hand and His will and purpose had predestined should occur!*

God Can and Will Use Any Kind of King

In the case of Cyrus, it was prophesied by Isaiah and Jeremiah that the children of Israel would return to Jerusalem. Who fulfilled that prophecy? A king of a pagan nation did! We know that people prayed and prophets prophesied, but the one who actually facilitated God's plan coming to pass was Cyrus.

In Isaiah chapter 53 it was prophesied that Jesus would be wounded for our transgressions and bruised for our iniquities, that the chastisement of our peace would be upon Him, and that by His stripes we would be healed. We see these wonderful prophecies about the great redemptive work of the Lord Jesus Christ. But who was going to actually physically carry them out?

Jesus was a good Man, a wonderful Man. Who would ever lay a finger on such a Man? Who would have the wickedness and a heart vile enough to kill one like Him? Who would even be authorized to order the torture and death by crucifixion which was required for the fulfilling of these prophecies?

A "David" kind of king would never have commissioned the death of Jesus. Neither would a "Cyrus" type of king. They would have let Jesus go because He was innocent.

However, what would have happened if Jesus had been let go? The prophecies would not have been fulfilled and we would all be unredeemed and on our way to hell along with all the other humans who ever lived on the face of the earth.

This prophecy had to be fulfilled and accomplished by a wicked king. It is interesting that God even figures wicked people into His plan: *"GOD made everything with a place and purpose; even the wicked are included—but for judgment"* (Prov. 16:4 Message).

To fulfill God's plan, Jesus had to be crucified, and only the Roman government had the authority to carry this out. It wasn't the Chief Priest and religious leaders, although they played their part. It could not have been just someone on the street; they wouldn't have the authority. It was precisely Herod and Pontius Pilate, just as Acts 4:27 states.

Remember when Pontius Pilate said to Jesus, "Why don't You say something? I can have You released! I have the power to say that You are innocent and get You off this charge"?

Jesus replied, "You don't have any power except what God gave you" (John 19:11).

So was God confused or slack regarding who He allowed to be put in office at that time in history? No! It all worked into His plan and purpose.

God's Plan Will Be Accomplished

Some prayers will remove leaders from office who will not submit to God's plan. Some prayers will put others *into* office to accomplish a particular divine assignment. There are some people who will not leave their office until they accomplish what is destined of them.

A good king would not have done what Herod and Pontius Pilate were destined to do. In our day, the same thing applies to kings and those in authority who are hard-hearted rulers. If they had a soft heart at all they would yield to God. Instead, their hearts remain hard.

You can pray for these people, even compassionately, but if they continue to resist God they become more cruel and irrational. Even with this category of wicked kings, prayer is to be persistently made. In this case, we are not called to change a king, but to prepare a way for our King!

Ultimately, even wicked kings cannot hold back the effects of persistent, Spirit-directed prayers. That is why He who sits in the heavens laughs even when kings are plotting against Him. Pharaoh, Herod, and Pontius Pilate didn't help prepare the way of the Lord by their goodness, but their roles actually became a part of the road.

> It is God who sets kings in place, and with our prayers each one will fulfill God's plan and purpose.

Let us not draw back from praying for any kind of king or ruler. It is God who sets kings in place, and with our prayers each one will fulfill God's plan and purpose as we prepare the way of the Lord (Dan. 2:20–22, Rom. 13:1–5).

~~~~~~~~~

CHAPTER 7

By Wisdom Kings Rule

"Therefore I exhort first of all that supplica-
tions, prayers, intercessions, and giving of
thanks be made for all men, for kings and all
who are in authority, that we may lead a
quiet and peaceable life in all godliness and
reverence. For this is good and acceptable in
the sight of God our Savior, who desires all
men to be saved and to come to
the knowledge of the truth."

—1 Timothy 2:1–4

We are instructed in First Timothy 2:1–4 to pray, make supplications, and give thanks for kings and all who are in authority. Since we have been instructed to do so, it would be reasonable to say we have also been authorized and commissioned by God to pray these prayers. So what do we pray for? What do we ask for on behalf of these kings and all in authority?

Proverbs 8:15 gives us a clue as to what is necessary for kings and all in authority to rule and govern rightly:

PROVERBS 8:15-16 (KJV)

15 BY ME [WISDOM] KINGS REIGN, and princes decree justice.

16 By me princes rule, and nobles, even all the judges of the earth.

A king known for wisdom is Solomon. Solomon was his father David's choice among all of his sons to succeed him on the throne. Most importantly, he was God's choice.

> *Of all the things Solomon could have asked of Almighty God, he chose wisdom to rule and judge correctly.*

Solomon had a dream in which God appeared to him and asked him to request anything he wanted. Of all the things Solomon could have asked of Almighty God, he chose wisdom to rule and judge correctly. He recognized that even though he was God's choice as king, he still needed God's wisdom to rule worthily. God was pleased with Solomon's request and granted him unparalleled wisdom. So pleased was God with this amazing request that he even gave Solomon the things he didn't request in addition to wisdom.

Solomon's wisdom manifested in his ability to administer the affairs of state (1 Kings 4:1–28), in surpassing the wisdom of other world leaders (1 Kings 4:30, 34), his composition of songs and poetry (1 Kings 4:32), and his extensive understanding of the natural world (1 Kings 4:33).

The first demonstration of God's gift of supreme wisdom was in direct answer to Solomon's prayer to be judicially wise. This wisdom caused Israel to be in awe of him as they recognized God's wisdom in him to do justice (1 Kings 3:16–28).

Two Sources of Wisdom

To Solomon, it was clear that in order to rule and reign justly in his kingdom, divine wisdom was necessary. This is true for the king of any nation, as well as for all who are in positions of authority. The Bible speaks of two sources of wisdom.

> *W*e know there is a wisdom from God or from above, but there is also wisdom which is from the earth or from below.

We know there is a wisdom from God or from above, but there is also wisdom which is from the earth or from below (Isa. 29:14, 1 Cor. 2:5).

Even though the wisdom which is from below is not as high as the wisdom of God, it is wisdom nonetheless and does have influence and effect.

Where did earthly wisdom come from? Let's look at Ezekiel 28. In this passage, Ezekiel is talking to the King of Tyre, who is referred to as a created being, not a man. Many theologians agree that this passage is referring to Lucifer and I would certainly agree with that interpretation.

EZEKIEL 28:12 (KJV)

12 Thus saith the Lord God; Thou sealest up the sum, full of wisdom, and perfect in beauty.

EZEKIEL 28:16–17 (Amplified)

16 Through the abundance of your commerce you were filled with lawlessness and violence, and you sinned; therefore I cast you out as a profane thing from the mountain of God and the guardian cherub drove you out from the midst of the stones of fire.

17 Your heart was proud and lifted up because of your beauty; you corrupted your wisdom for the sake of your splendor. I cast you to the ground; I lay you before kings, that they might gaze at you.

When God created Lucifer, He made him perfect in wisdom. Lucifer didn't lose his wisdom when he was lifted up with pride and fell; the perfect wisdom which he was created with became corrupted. Now the wisdom which comes from below is this corrupted wisdom from Lucifer, or Satan, himself. It is with corrupt wisdom that he has built his house and rules the kingdom of darkness, a perversion of Proverbs 24:3.

There is a wisdom which is pure and has remained perfect through the ages. It is the wisdom from God and is available to us as believers, as His sons and daughters. This wisdom comes directly from God, is made accessible to us by Jesus, and is transmitted to us through the ministry of the Holy Spirit (1 Cor. 2:12–13).

The following scriptures contrast the wisdom which is from below and the wisdom which is from above:

1 CORINTHIANS 2:6 (KJV)

6 Howbeit we speak wisdom among them that are perfect: yet not the wisdom of this world, nor of the princes of this world, that come to nought . . .

JAMES 3:15, 17

15 This wisdom does not descend from above, but is earthly, sensual, demonic.

17 But the wisdom that is from above is first pure, then peaceable, gentle, willing to yield, full of mercy and good fruits, without partiality and without hypocrisy.

Clearly, there are two kinds of wisdom from two opposite sources. One comes from below and is corrupt; the other is perfect and comes from above, from God.

When filling your vehicle with fuel at a service station, many times there are two to four varieties of fuel to choose from. The kind of fuel you put in your vehicle will affect the performance of the engine. In the same way, Proverbs 8:15 says by wisdom kings reign. It would be obvious that of the two types of wisdom contrasted in James, the wisdom from above would be the best wisdom by which kings and all who are in authority should operate.

It is by wisdom that kings reign and decree justice, rulers rule, judges judge, and nobles declare law. But the question is, which wisdom is fueling them? Is it the wisdom Satan corrupted when he was cast out of the mountain of God, or is it divine wisdom? The wisdom used will definitely determine the performance.

> (W)isdom of either type will make a leader convincing.

Proverbs 16:23 says, "*The mind of the wise instructs his mouth, and adds learning and persuasiveness to his lips*" (Amplified). Can even corrupt wisdom possess persuasiveness? Wisdom of either type will make a leader convincing. Wisdom, though it may be evil, will make the man who possesses it persuasive (1 Cor. 1:17, 1 Cor. 2:4).

Let's take Adolf Hitler for instance. He was very persuasive. Some referred to him as charismatic or gifted. He persuaded a whole nation and beyond, and thousands of people blindly believed in him. It was wisdom which added persuasiveness to his lips. Obviously, it was not wisdom from above. The wisdom by which he ruled came from beneath!

Supreme Wisdom

There is a higher wisdom available to us as believers and children of the Most High God (Prov. 3:4–7). It is supremely higher, smarter, and more powerful and persuasive than the wisdom from below.

1 CORINTHIANS 2:7-8

7 But we speak the wisdom of God in a mystery, the hidden wisdom which God ordained before the ages for our glory,

8 which none of the rulers of this age knew; for had they known, they would not have crucified the Lord of glory.

In prayer, we are working with God Who is superior to all. For us to pray in such a way as to insinuate that the devil is only a shade lower than God would be extremely uninformed and rude. God is exceedingly wise. The Bible calls Him the only wise God (1 Tim. 1:17, Jude 1:25). There is much in the Word of God concerning God's wisdom. It is to be sought as the "principle thing" (Prov. 4:7). Wisdom is something we are actually instructed to call out for (Prov. 7:4).

Paul prayed that the believers in Ephesus would be filled with all wisdom and knowledge (Eph. 1:17). He said that he prayed that without ceasing. He also prayed that they would be filled with the knowledge of the will of God in all wisdom and spiritual understanding (Col. 1:9). These scriptural prayers emphasize the importance of God's wisdom to each of us.

The Bible says that Jesus Himself has been made unto us wisdom (1 Cor. 1:30). If we have Christ and He is our wisdom, is there a need to ask for it? Asking is actually

> Asking [for wisdom] is actually one of the ways to appropriate what has been given to us in Christ.

one of the ways to appropriate what has been given to us in Christ. James 1:5 says that if any of you lack wisdom, let him ask. James says further in chapter 4, verse 2, that you have not because you don't ask.

Your spiritual shelves are stocked full of wisdom but it must be taken hold of. When you ask for wisdom, you appropriate it. You "take it off the shelf" in order to operate in it. In asking for it, you acknowledge that there is a wisdom that is not yours and is not human, a wisdom which actually makes all human wisdom pale. Paul said that human wisdom is foolishness with God (1 Cor. 3:19).

God's Wisdom Dispensed Through the Church

> If no request is made for divine wisdom by which to rule, then by default, the only wisdom left for [rulers] is the wisdom from below.

There are rulers who pray and ask for God's wisdom. But what about those who don't? We are to ask God on their behalf to give them wisdom. If no request is made for divine wisdom by which to rule, then by default, the only wisdom left for them is the wisdom from below.

In response to the instruction of First Timothy 2:1–2 to pray for kings, one thing we can request is that wisdom be given to them. God has promised to give it liberally. And when we ask, let's ask in faith, nothing wavering. Rather than trying to figure out what the king is supposed to do relating to national and eternal affairs, let's absolutely trust the Holy Spirit. Remember, God's plan does not only affect the well being of a nation; but His plan is ultimately designed to prepare for a harvest of souls (1 Tim. 2:4).

God's wisdom orchestrated the events and government when Jesus was crucified. Put yourself in the disciples' sandals. Every detail of the unjust hearing, the flogging, and the crucifixion looked terribly wrong to them. It looked like a disaster to the plan of God, when actually each detail was impeccably and precisely orchestrated by God's wisdom. Could it be that there are events to occur before Jesus' Second Coming which appear to be contrary to the plan of God, but actually facilitate the plan perfectly?

God's will is to exhibit His wisdom through the Church, not independent of the Church. In fact, if the demonic principalities and powers are going to know the many aspects of God's wisdom, it will be because the Church receives wisdom from God and displays and dispenses it in the world.

EPHESIANS 3:10 (Amplified)

10 [The purpose is] that through the church the complicated, many-sided wisdom of God in all its infinite variety and innumerable aspects might now be made known to the angelic rulers and authorities (principalities and powers) in the heavenly sphere.

> In prayer we can appropriate and dispense this wisdom directly to kings or to those who surround them.

Consistent prayer in this area keeps a steady supply of divine wisdom for rulers to draw upon. In prayer we can appropriate and dispense this wisdom directly to kings or to those who surround them. No matter what things seem like, let us be encouraged not to withhold our prayers, but to continue—full of faith and led by the Holy Spirit.

With God as the Mastermind behind our strategy in these days, there will be absolutely no possible way for defeat. There is no way we are going to lose. There is no way we will miss the harvest.

There is also no way the devil can trap you if you tap in to the wisdom of God. If he thinks he has you trapped, the superior strategy of God will actually work toward his undoing—the cross being the classic example. In Jesus' death, the devil thought, "Oh, I got Him! I got Him!" But the very moment it looked the worst was when the enemy was in fact defeated.

Let's not give God any weak praying. Let's rise up and see what our potential is in prayer. We have the advantage because we have God's supreme wisdom available to us. Let's lay hold of it and dispense it in prayer!

CHAPTER 8

When the Righteous Are in Authority

"When the righteous are in authority, the people rejoice; But when a wicked man rules, the people groan."

—Proverbs 29:2

There are two ways we can interpret this scripture, and both are correct. First, it is certainly true that when godly people are leading a country, the wise and just decisions they make are a cause for the people to rejoice. The same is true when godly people are in any position of authority, for that matter. The Holy Spirit often leads us to pray that godly people rise to these places of government.

We have also seen, and will further discover in this chapter, that having a godly person in a position of authority does not guarantee right decisions will be made. Leaders must have a supply of divine wisdom by which to rule. Again, this is where prayer comes in. Another way to look at this scripture is to take the meaning from each word literally. Let's look at the verse again.

"When the righteous . . ." Who are the righteous? As born-again believers, we are righteous (2 Cor. 5:21).

> When believers are exercising their blood-purchased authority, God's purposes on the earth advance.

". . . are in authority . . ." We've established the fact that Jesus has given us a place of authority. Moreover, it is imperative that we are conscious of and *exercise* that authority in prayer and in our lives. When we do, we have the same effect as Moses did when he raised his rod on the mountain and the Israelites prevailed. When believers are exercising their blood-purchased authority, God's purposes on the earth advance.

If a nation has a godly king, but the believers in that land are lax in *their* responsibility to dispense God's rule, the godly king will stagger in his office and be vulnerable to the wisdom of the world. The result can be ungodly and foolish decisions which negatively affect the people.

On the other hand, if a nation with an ungodly leader is blessed with believers who not only know their rights and authority, but exercise them in prayer for that leader, there will be supernatural intervention for the general good of the people in that nation. Divine intervention would be reflected on a natural level in areas such as education, social justice, and economy, bringing about a quiet and peaceable life in all godliness and honesty (1 Tim. 2:2).

God has changed and can still change a whole system of government to accommodate the increase of His Kingdom, resulting in a harvest of souls, when the Church prays. Ultimately, if the Church stands

> If the Church stands in its place of authority and does its job, there will be cause in any country for rejoicing.

in its place of authority and does its job, there will be cause in any country for rejoicing, both naturally and spiritually.

The Government Shall Be Upon His Shoulder

To bring more clarity on this matter, let me ask you a couple of the same questions the Holy Spirit posed to me for the purpose of leading me into truth.

Who is the Head of the Church? Jesus, of course. Where are the shoulders—on the head or on the body? Certainly the shoulders are a part of the body. Shoulders speak of responsibility. With that in mind, let's look at this familiar verse:

ISAIAH 9:6

6 For unto us a Child is born, Unto us a Son is given; And the government will be upon His shoulder. And His name will be called Wonderful, Counselor, Mighty God, Everlasting Father, Prince of Peace.

> God's intervention in governments is limited to the action the Church takes.

Notice, the government rests upon His shoulder. In other words, the government shall rest upon His Body, and the Body of Christ is the Church. We as the Church are to uphold the government. To be sure, there are various ways of interpreting this verse, but picturing the government resting on the shoulders of the Body of Christ helps us grasp the fact that the Church has a responsibility to pray and utilize its God-given authority. God's intervention in governments is limited to the action the Church takes. The welfare of the government is our responsibility.

For example, in 1979 Kenneth E. Hagin had a vision in which Jesus said to him, "If the Christians of this nation had done what I told them to do in My Word and had prayed for the leaders of their country, they could have kept those evil spirits you saw in 1970 from operating in this nation. None of those upheavals would have occurred in your nation. You would *not* have had the political, social, and economic disturbances in this nation, and the President never would have made the mistakes he made. In fact, I'm holding the Church responsible for the President's mistakes."[1]

This is the order of God! The Church is not *under* the state, or the government. The Church is under the Head. We are the Body of Christ, and the Body of Christ is positioned far above all principality, power, might, and dominion of demon spirit or office of man.

Praying from any other position will make you apologetic or at best hopeful. Ephesians 6:17 says we have *"the sword of the Spirit, which is the word of God"* as an offensive weapon in our prayer armor. Praying with unbelief and wishful thinking dulls your sword.

There is a difference between Church and state. The Church is not to look to the government for supply as much as it is to give Heaven's supply of anointing through the prophets to the kings and military leaders. The Church is to dispense the anointing which is necessary for the government to do the job God wants it to do.

> The Church is to dispense the anointing which is necessary for the government to do the job God wants it to do.

As we who have been made righteous realize and take our spiritual position of authority, which is right under the Head, the people will have a reason to rejoice.

---

[1] Kenneth E. Hagin, *The Triumphant Church* (Tulsa: Faith Library Publications, 1993), 236. Used by permission.

———

CHAPTER 9

For Such a Time as This

*"For if you remain completely silent at this
time, relief and deliverance will arise for the
Jews from another place, but you and your
father's house will perish. Yet who knows
whether you have come to the kingdom FOR
SUCH A TIME AS THIS?"*

—Esther 4:14

This verse has been used extensively as a great source of inspiration. It is in harmony with other verses of scripture which speak of God's purpose and destiny for each of us as members of the Body of Christ. However, this verse was written specifically about a queen who came into a position of authority and direct influence to the king.

Esther came into the position of queen *"for such a time as this."* What was *"such a time as this"*?

Let's imagine! How wonderful it would be to take a whole month to soak in a bathtub filled with special oils and perfumes, to have access to a queen's wardrobe, to live in an elegant palace, to feast on delicious gourmet food, and to have servants to do everything for you! How wonderful would that be! Esther grew up as an orphaned girl, but now she's a queen!

But why did Esther become queen? Did she come into the kingdom for such a time as *this*—splendor and ease?

Actually, this time of which Mordecai spoke to Esther was a time of impending annihilation of the Jewish people. This was the precise time for which she became queen!

> [God] purposefully brings people to positions of authority who are best suited for the time.

God knows the plans of the devil in advance. He purposefully brings people to positions of authority who are best suited for the time. At first they may not understand their divine purpose for being in authority. They may think they came to that political or military or otherwise influential position for a totally different reason. Then something happens which gives them a defining moment. Perhaps someone speaks into their lives as Mordecai spoke to Esther, and it dawns on them, "Oh, *this* is what I'm here for!"

Esther enjoyed dressing up like a queen and appreciated all the advantages of her position until her husband, the king, issued a proclamation for the extermination of her people. Suddenly she became more aware of her *responsibility and purpose* for being queen than she was of all the glamour and personal benefits.

Esther responded: " '*GO, GATHER ALL THE JEWS WHO ARE PRESENT IN SHUSHAN, AND FAST FOR ME; neither eat nor drink for three days, night or day. My maids and I will fast likewise. And so I will go to the king, which is against the law; and if I perish, I perish!* ' " (Esther 4:16).

When Esther gave this instruction to Mordecai, she was in essence saying, "Okay, cousin Mordecai, I'm here. I am the queen. I understand that nobody else is closer to the king than I. But now *you* go get all of God's people together and have them fast for me."

In order for the plan of God to be put into action, Queen Esther wasn't the only one to play a vital role. All the Jews in Shushan fasted three days for her! This part of the story beautifully depicts the flow of Heaven's supply of wisdom, grace, and strength which comes through the prayers of God's people to those who have been placed in positions of natural authority.

In answer to prayer, Esther received courage to risk her life on her people's behalf. As the story unfolds, we see her operating under the influence of such divine wisdom and favor that the king not only granted her access into his presence, but promised her up to half his kingdom!

Queen Esther was able to fulfill her destiny and save the Jewish people from annihilation (hence, the ancestral line through which the Messiah would come), not just because she was queen, but because she was backed up with prayer.

> *A*bdication of our position puts the welfare of the government and nation at risk.

It is important to pray for the right people to come into positions of authority during critical times. But it is grossly irresponsible, after having fervently prayed a person into a position of authority, to then resort to a passive, apathetic mode, saying, "Now you work for us. Do a good job for us." Abdication of our position puts the welfare of the government and nation at risk.

Even with the right person in authority, we must remember that the government is not itself the highest authority.

> *G*overnmental authority is not the highest position of authority which can be occupied by the righteous.

The government rests upon the shoulders of the Body of Christ. The Church is to carry the government.

In fact, governmental authority is not the highest

position of authority which can be occupied by the righteous. The highest authority is the Throne of God, and we have been raised to sit at God's right hand in Christ.

In the story of Esther, God's purposes were accomplished through the person of His choosing in a position of natural authority and God's people who were *simultaneously* operating in their place of authority.

To the Church and Through the Church

Prophecies are going to come to pass in these days. We will be able to watch them on the news broadcast of our choice. Many of these prophecies will not be fulfilled by the Church directly. They will, however, be fulfilled by the Church praying. Anointing, power, direction, and influence from God will be issued through our prayers to people in authority: kings, leaders, people of influence, people in civic authority, and military people.

Through prayer, the Church will issue and dispense the anointing by which these people will fulfill the prophecies, in much the same way that Elijah and Elisha dispensed the anointing.

> Through prayer, the Church will issue and dispense the anointing by which these people will fulfill the prophecies.

Just what is our potential in prayer? What are the capabilities? What can God do when we pray for kings and all who are in authority? Sometimes the kings we pray for may not be men after God's heart like King David. They may be a "Cyrus" kind of king or even a "Pharaoh" kind of king. Nevertheless, God can do amazing things with our prayers when we obey what is said in First Timothy 2:1–2.

Proverbs 21:1 says that God can turn the heart of a king. When we pray, God communicates with leaders and influences them in a variety of ways.

One way God speaks is through dreams. King Nebuchadnezzar had a dream which made him sick and unable to eat or sleep (Dan. chapter 4). Pharaoh had a dream which only Joseph could interpret, positioning Joseph as second in the kingdom (Gen. chapter 41).

God confused the counsel which was to be given to King Ahab so he did the wrong thing. God arranged for him to believe stupid counsel (2 Chron. chapter 18). The same thing happened with Absalom: he believed the wrong counsel (2 Sam. chapter 17). Originally, these men had dangerous plans, but their schemes were foiled when they believed wrong counsel. Do you see what tremendous advantage we have as we work together with God?

In the case of King Ahasuerus, God used a beautiful young Jewish girl backed by prayer. Haman's wicked scheme was sabotaged and a "road was built" for God's glory to be manifested.

God also used unusual signs and wonders. What about writing on the wall? That would get the king's attention, as it did in Daniel chapter 5.

A divine appearance of Jesus Himself changed one man of great authority by the name of Saul into Paul the Apostle and writer of most of the New Testament letters (Acts chapter 9).

Too often, we only pray for those in authority when circumstances relating to our government begin to crowd in on our lives to threaten or hinder our happiness. Even so, this may not evoke a prayer, but a complaint.

We are not called to complain; we are called to reign! And not just until the situation is tolerable and then stop. We are to earnestly continue reigning, so

> We are not called to complain; we are called to reign!

that more is brought about than just happiness and ease to our personal lives. With the Holy Spirit's leading, we can be more precise, focused, and effectual in our praying, making tremendous power available for God's plans to prevail in the earth in these last days.

Let's be inspired to pray and do our part in preparing the way of the Lord. Surely we, too, have been brought to the Kingdom *for such a time as this!*

Why should you consider attending
RHEMA
Bible Training Center?

Here are a few good reasons:

- Training at one of the top Spirit-filled Bible schools anywhere

- Teaching based on steadfast faith in God's Word

- Growth in your spiritual walk coupled with practical training in effective ministry

- Specialization in the area of your choosing: Youth or Children's Ministry, Evangelism, Pastoral Care, Missions, Biblical Studies, or Supportive Ministry

- Optional intensive third-year programs: School of Worship, School of Pastoral Ministry, School of World Missions, and General Extended Studies

- Worldwide ministry opportunities—while you're in school

- An established network of churches and ministries around the world who depend on RHEMA to supply full-time staff and support ministers

- A two-year evening school taught entirely in Spanish is also available. Log on to **www.cebrhema.org** for more information.

Call today for information or application material.
1-888-28-FAITH (1-888-283-2484)
www.rbtc.org

RHEMA Bible Training Center admits students of any race, color, or ethnic origin.

OFFER CODE—BKORD:PRMDRBTC

Word Partner Club

WORKING *together* TO REACH THE WORLD!

WPC
People. Power. Purpose.

Have you ever dropped a stone into water? Small waves rise up at the point of impact and travel in all directions. It's called a ripple effect. That's the kind of impact Christians are meant to have in this world—the kind of impact that the RHEMA family is producing in the earth today.

The Word Partner Club links Christians with a shared interest in reaching people with the Gospel and the message of faith in God.

Together we are reaching across generations, cultures, and nations to spread the Good News of Jesus Christ to every corner of the earth.

To join us in reaching the world,
visit **www.rhema.org/wpc** or call 1-866-312-0972

Always on.

For the latest news and information on products, media, podcasts, study resources, and special offers, visit us online 24 hours a day.